Let Me Touch the Sky

Valerie Bloom was born in 1956 in Jamaica, in a village called Orange Hill. She grew up and went to school in the nearby town of Frankfield.

Valerie has been a librarian, a teacher, a steel band instructor and an arts officer. She studied English, African and Caribbean literature and history at the University of Kent, and was awarded an honorary masters degree from the university in 1995.

Her first book of poetry, *Touch Mi, Tell Mi*, was published in 1983 and her first collection for children, *Duppy Jamboree*, in 1992. Other books for children include *Fruits; Ackee, Breadfruit, Callaloo* and *The World is Sweet*.

Valerie Bloom now writes, performs and conducts workshops full time.

D1004240

Other books by Valerie Bloom

Let Me Touch the Sky

Selected Poems for Children

Valerie Bloom

Illustrated by Kathy Lucas

MACMILLAN CHILDREN'S BOOKS

For Doug, with love

First published 2000 by Macmillan Children's Books

This edition published 2001 by Macmillan Children's Books
a division of Macmillan Publishers Ltd
25 Eccleston Place, London SW1W 9NF
Basingstoke and Oxford
www.macmillan.com

Associated companies throughout the world

ISBN 0 330 39216 6

3 5 7 9 8 6 4 2

A CIP catalogue record for this book is available from
the British Library.

Printed and bound in Great Britain by
Mackays of Chatham plc, Chatham, Kent

'Duppy Jamboree', 'Fruits', 'Don' go ova dere', 'Sun a-shine, rain a-fall',
'Chicken dinner', 'Tables', 'Sly mangoose' and 'Leave dem wasp alone'
first published in *Duppy Jamboree*, CUP 1992.

Contents

Autumn Gilt

The late September sunshine
Lime green on the linden leaves
Burns bronze on the slated roof-tops,
Yellow on the farmer's last sheaves.

It flares flame-like on the fire hydrant,
Is ebony on the blackbird's wing,
Blue beryl on the face of the ocean,
Glints gold on the bride's wedding ring.

A sparkling rainbow on the stained-glass window,
It's a silver sheen on the kitchen sink,
The late September sunshine
Is a chameleon, I think.

When Granny

Song-bird shut dem mout' an lissen,
Church bell don't bother to ring,
All de little stream keep quiet
When mi Granny sing.

De sun up in de sky get jealous,
Him wish him got her style,
For de whole place full o' brightness
When mi Granny smile.

First a happy soun' jus' bubblin'
From her belly, low an' sof',
Den a thunderclap o' merriment
When mi Granny laugh.

De tree dem start to swing dem branch dem,
Puss an' dawg begin to prance,
Everyt'ing ketch de happy fever
When mi Granny dance.

Everybody look out fe Granny
Mek sure dat she satisfy,
For de whole worl' full o' sadness
When mi Granny cry.

Haircut Rap

Ah sey, ah want it short,
Short back an' side,
Ah tell him man, ah tell him
When ah teck him aside,
Ah sey, ah want a haircut
Ah can wear with pride,
So lef' it long on top
But short back an' side.

Ah sey try an' put a pattern
In the shorter part,
Yuh could put a skull an' crossbone,
Or an arrow through a heart,
Meck sure ah have enough hair lef'
Fe cover me wart,
Lef' a likkle pon the top,
But the res' – keep it short.

Well, bwoy, him start to cut
An' me settle down to wait,
Him was cuttin' from seven
Till half-past eight,
Ah was startin' to get worried
'Cause ah see it gettin' late,
But then him put the scissors down
Sey, 'There yuh are, mate.'

Well ah did see a skull an' a
Criss-cross bone or two,
But was me own skull an' bone
That was peepin' through
Ah look jus' like a monkey
Ah did see once at the zoo,
Him sey, 'What's de matter, Tammy,
Don't yuh like the hair-do?'

Well, ah feel me heart stop beatin'
When ah look pon me reflection,
Ah feel like somet'ing frizzle up
Right in me middle section
Ah look aroun' fe somewhey
Ah could crawl into an' hide
The day ah mek me brother cut
Me hair short back an' side.

Swinging

Push me, Mummy, push me
High up in the air,
Higher, Mummy, higher,
Send me over there

Where that branch is growing,
This is so much fun!
Let me touch those leaves, Mummy,
Let me touch the sun.

Swing me, Mummy, swing me,
Do you call this high?
Let me touch that house there, Mummy,
Let me touch the sky.

Stop me, Mummy, stop me,
Get me off this swing!
My ears are popping, Mummy,
My head is starting to ring.

Oh the ground is spinning!
I think I'm going to die.
Really, Mummy, why did you
Push the swing so high?

Clouds

Little bits of cloud
High in the sky,
Little bits of cloud
Float slowly by,
Count all the bits
And that will be,
The number of fishes
There are in the sea.

The Camel

The camel's feet are soft, wide, and
Two-toed, for walking in the sand.
His nostrils close when the desert wind blows,
To keep the sand from out his nose.
His lashes are long, the perfect size,
For keeping sand out of his eyes.
He has a hump, which is quite good
For long desert journeys without food.
It stores the fat for him you see,
And he uses this in an emergency.
The camel's designed for the desert, it's true,
That's why we keep him in a zoo.

Fox and Rabbits

Rabbits munching, nose a-twitch,
Fox a-prowling by the ditch
Behind the hedgerows where the
Rabbits munch.

Rabbits pausing, ears alert,
Fox a-crouching in the dirt,
Heavy with the birds he had
For lunch.

Rabbits standing, sniff the wind,
Fox is ready, determined
To catch some baby rabbits for
His tea.

Rabbits' ears perk up to hear
Fox a-crawling, well aware
That surprise and timing are
The key.

Rabbits running, swift as sight,
Fox is leaping into flight,
But alas, fox was not born
With wings.

Fox is sitting in the ditch,
Contemplating the price which
Hunting rabbits on a full
Stomach brings.

Barry and de Duppy

Barry meet up pon one duppy one night really late,
The duppy look pon Barry and him say to himself, 'Great!
Ah going to have some fun with this little bwoy tonight,
Ah going to jump out front o' him an' give him such
    a fright.'

Barry see the duppy standing there beside the tree,
Barry say, 'Mmn hmm, me brother come to frighten me,
Ah going to have some fun with him, ah going to act
    real cool,
Him no know say dat I know today is April fool.'

The duppy jump out front o' Barry, an' him bawl out, 'Boo!'
Barry never budge, the duppy halla out 'oo-ooo-oo!'
Barry ask the duppy, 'Wait a minute, yuh can't see?
What yuh mean by who? Yuh no see say that is me?'

The duppy really surprise, but him naw give up so quick
Him twist him head, it pop off o' him shoulder with
    a click,
Him hold it out to Barry and say, 'Hold me head fe me,'
But Barry didn' notice, him looking at a cotton tree.

'See that cotton tree? Me hear say nuff duppy live there,'
The duppy start fe wonder how this bwoy so hard fe scare,
Him put him head back on and moan, 'And me live in
    there too-oo.'
Barry say, 'eh eh, massa, seems like yuh got the flu.

Yuh better come to bed.' And Barry walking down the lane,
The duppy start fe howl like say him in a dreadful pain.
'Yuh want fe raise the dead?' say Barry. 'Massa, what
    do yuh?'
A now the duppy perplex, him say, 'this bwoy mad fe true!'

Barry say, 'Yuh trying hard fe bus people eardrum?
Mama must be wondering where yuh is, yuh better come.'
The duppy halla, 'No sah, me naw go nowhey with him.'
Him float up to the cotton tree, perch pon the highest limb.

Barry never see, for him walking on, real cool,
Satisfy say that him make him brother look a fool,
Him feeling really happy, but poor Barry nearly dead,
When him find out all this time him brother fast asleep
    in bed.

Duppy Jamboree

'Back to back, belly to belly
Ah don't care at all
For me done dead a'ready.
Back to back, belly to belly
In de duppy jamboree.'

What that noise me hearing
Coming from out o' doah?
Mi get out o' bed, pull back de curtain
An' peep out tru de window.

Me rub me yeye an' look again,
Can't believe wha me just see,
Twenty-seven duppy dere
Staring back at me!

One o' dem stand up dere
With him head under him arm,
One o' dem is a big ole bull
Like de one pon Granpa farm.

But this one's yeye dem full o' fire,
An' it have on one big ole chain,
Is a rollin-calf! Me shet me yeye,
Den open dem again

When me hear dem singing.
Me open me yeye wide
Ah think one have a horse head
Growing from him side!

De Devil out deh with dem
With him cow-foot an' him horn,
Him long tail wrap right roun him wais'
Him pitchfork in him han'.

Lawd, him looking up at me!
Him see me! Him a grin!
It look like sey him come
To punish me for all me sin.

Dem comin to de doorway,
Me noh ready yet fe dead!
Me fly into me mama room
An' jump into her bed.

Yeye-water runnin' dung me face
Till me can hardly see,
'De duppy dem out o' doah, Mama,
Doan mek dem come ketch me!'

Mama hold me tight an' laugh,
'Noh mek dem frighten you,
Is not a duppy jamboree,
Is just de Jonkunnu.'

Christmas Eve

Listen to de fee-fee, Janey!
Hear de whistle dem a-blow?
Hear de way de fire crackers
Bus out loud, loud, outa doah?

Watch dem runnin' wid de starlight!
Watch de balloon dem a-fly!
Watch de way de rocket dem
Jus' brighten up de sky!

Listen, Janey, hear dah soun?
Dat's de Jonkunnu coming now,
Listen to de fife an' drum dem,
Look through de window, see de cow?

See de devil an' de horsehead?
See de belly woman too?
Run, Janey, gi' dem a ten cent,
Quick before dem trouble yuh.

Pay dem for de music, Janey,
Show dem sey yuh like de soun',
Ef yuh fraid de devil pitchfork
Throw de ten cent pon de groun'.

Hear de people shoutin 'Chrismus!'
Every time a balloon bus?
Everybody buying, buying,
Dose who don' have money, trus.

An' what a crowd pon de street, Janey,
Not a vehicle coulda pass,
People hole dem pickney tight
For ef dem let dem go, dem los'.

Hear de clock a strike eleven,
Come on, Janey, one hour still
Before de shop dem shut, so galang,
Put on yuh sweater 'gainst de night chill.

Galang, Janey, why yuh crying?
Dis is not de time fe sorrow,
Jus' push me bed nearer de winda,
Now gwan, chile, Christmas Day tomorrow.

Christmas is Here

When the fee-fees start to bloom
Purple and white,
When the days begin to be
Shorter than night,
When the poinsettia's leaves
Turn from green to red,
When the turkey in the coop
Starts to look well-fed,
When we dig the yellow yams,
And pick the gungo peas,
When the tall, white, cane-flags
Start waving in the breeze,
When oranges and tangerines
Start to fill the baskets
Of the people on their way
To the different markets,
When the fruits which have been dried
Are soaking in the wine,
When the fat green cho-chos hang
Heavy from the vine,
When we look out on the fields
To the red bulbs of sorrel,
When the pickled meats come out
From their place in the brine barrel,
When each meal contains a slice
Of avocado pear,
Then we know for certain that
Christmas-time is here.

Granny Is

Granny is
fried dumplin' an' run-dung,
coconut drops an' grater cake,
fresh ground coffee smell in the mornin'
when we wake.

Granny is
loadin' up the donkey,
basket full on market day
with fresh snapper the fishermen bring back
from the bay.

Granny is
clothes washin' in the river
scrubbin' dirt out on the stone
haulin' crayfish an' eel from water
on her own.

Granny is
stories in the moonlight
underneath the guangu tree
and a spider web of magic
all round we.

Granny say,
'Only de best fe de gran'children,
it don' matter what de price,
don't want no one pointin' finger.'

Granny nice.

Who Dat Girl?

Who dat wide-eye likkle girl
Staring out at me?
Wid her hair in beads an' braids
An' skin like ebony?

Who dat girl, her eye dem bright
Like night-time peeny-wallie?
Wid Granny chain dem circle roun'
Her ankle, neck, an' knee?

Who dat girl in Mummy's shoes,
Waist tie wid Dad's hankie?
Who dat girl wid teeth like pearl
Who grinning out at me?

Who dat girl? Who dat girl?
Pretty as poetry?
Who dat girl in de lookin'-glass?

Yuh mean dat girl is me?

Longsight Market

Buy yuh ripe banana! Fresh callaloo!
Buy yuh yellow heart breadfruit! Fiiiiish!

How much a poun' fe yuh yellow yam?
Massa, don't talk rubbish!
A gold yuh yellow yam make out of?
Then how yuh sell de saltfish?

Yuh see yuh, hell won't miss yuh,
For yuh such a bareface t'ief!
Put it back, me not a millionaire.
Make me see that tin o' corn beef.

A from when yuh have dem yam here?
Must be from de year o' nought,
Make has'e, take it, oh yuh have red peas,
Make me see it, how much a quart?

How yuh want to get rich quick so?
Yuh not afraid yuh go to jail?
Yuh can get t'ree year fe robbery yuh know!
What a-pound for de pig's tail?

Yuh face look like a eighty pence!
Move yuhself, but man, yuh hard!
Look pon de plantain that de man a-sell!
Yuh no shame fe carry dem from yuh yahd?

Dem plantain will give people consumption,
Dem not even fit fe hag,
Keep quiet! Don't yuh hurry me,
Yuh got brown rice? How much a bag?

That don' sound too bad, make me see it,
No, Massa, this rice too dirty!
Beg yuh sell me half o' that bun dere,
How yuh mean yuh can't cut i'?

Lissen, man, just stop yuh noise,
Ah don't want nobody to hurry me,
Me have to make sure me get good t'ings
For me work too hard for me two quatty.

People a-wait? Make dem stan' dere,
Beg yuh sell me one o' dem cho-cho,
How dem yah green banana look sick so?
An' beg yuh sell me one bag o' toto.

What a way de mango dem fubba-fubba?
Unoo won' stop sell t'ings force-ripe?
An' look how de sweet potato dem twis'-up,
Like when jackass have gripe.

Alright, dat will do for today,
How yuh mean if 'that is all?'
That is all yes – wait one minute,
Make me see that tin o' Milo by de wall.

Alright, me see it, now put it back,
Now add up fe me, this an' that,
Yuh can stay dere ask for one pound
For is fifty pence me gat.

Well yuh shouldn' sell so dear,
Stop, yuh don't have no sweet corn?
An' me did want two corn fe buy, yuh know,
Here, me will give yuh de balance next week, me gawn.

Buy yuh ripe banana! Fresh callaloo!
Buy yuh yellow heart breadfruit! Fiiiiish!

Sleepless Lamb

'I cannot sleep!' the little lamb cried.
'I can't sleep though I've tried and tried.'
'I'll tell you a secret,' his mother said,
'Remember, when you go to bed,
Lambs who want to fall asleep'll
Do so best by counting people.'

Tall Tales

I saw a silver mermaid
With green and purple hair,
I saw her sitting by the river
In her underwear.

No, you never, you never.

I did.

I saw a rolling-calf
With twenty-seven toes,
I saw the smoke and fire
That was coming from its nose.

No, you never, you never.

I did.

I saw the devil dancing reggae
In the bright moonlight,
I saw him sting a donkey
With his tail the other night.

No, you never, you never.

I did.

I saw your father busy
Reading your report card,
I saw him looking for you
All around the yard.

No, you never. You never! You did!?

Football Blues

Ah never did wan' go to dat match,
Ah say ah will stay home an' watch
De TV. But same time ah catch,
De advert fe de half-price ticket.

So ah standin' dere in de freezin' cole,
Waitin' fe Matthews score a goal,
An' it really hurt me to me soul
When de bwoy miss.

But dat no nutten to de pain me feel
When Parkinson kick up him heel
An' like a elephant pon a banana peel,
Crash to de grung.

De crowd begin fe scream an' shout,
For Watson 'tan up eena de goal mout',
An' nobody don' have no doubt
Say him a-go score.

De ball sail way ova de bar,
Knock out a man a-park him car,
De odder side start to laugh, 'Har, har!'
An' me shame case burs'.

Nex' Smiley kick de ball, miss, instead
Kick Randall eena de back o' him head,
Randall start play like say him dead,
An' dem score a goal.

De odder side dem start go wile
Like a bush fire dat jus' smell ile,
Dem whoop an' shout, an' all dis while,
A one t'ing pon me min'.

Me 'tan up deh an' me coulda cry,
When me look pon de ticket me buy,
An' memba how much steak an' kidney pie
Me coulda get fe dat money.

Fruits

Half a pawpaw in the basket
Only one o' we can have it,
Wonder which one that will be?
I have a feeling that is me.

One guinep up in the tree
Hanging down there tempting me
It don't mek no sense to pick it,
One guinep can't feed a cricket.

Two ripe guava pon the shelf,
I know I hide them there meself,
When night come an' it get dark
Me an' them will have a talk.

Three sweet-sop, well I jus' might
Give one o' them a nice big bite,
Cover up the bite jus' so, sis,
Then no one will ever notice.

Four red apple near me chair,
Who so careless put them there?
Them don't know how me love apple?
Well, thank God fe silly people.

Five jew-plum, I can't believe it!
How they know jew-plum's me fav'rit?
But why they hide them in the cupboard?
Cho, people can be so awkward.

Six naseberry, you want a nibble?
Why baby must always dribble?
Come wipe you mout', it don't mek sense
To broadcast the evidence.

Seven mango! What a find
The smaddy who lef them really kind,
One fe you an' six fe me,
If you want more, climb the tree.

Eight orange fe cousin Clem,
But I have just one problem,
How to get rid o' the eight skin
That the orange them come in.

Nine jackfruit! Not even me
Can finish nine, but let me see,
I don't suppose that they will miss one,
That was hard, but now me done.

Ten banana, mek them stay,
I feeling really full today,
Mek me lie down on me bed, quick,
Lawd, ah feeling really sick.

The Election

The animals held a council
To elect themselves a king,
They wanted someone strong and bold,
Who could lead in everything,
The elephant was the council's choice,
Each member voted 'Yea!'
That is, each member but the horse,
Who loudly shouted, 'Neigh!'

The vote had to be unanimous,
That's what they had agreed,
They knew without the horse's vote
Their plan would not succeed,
They thought it was important
To crown the elephant right away,
They had the throne, the robe, the orb,
And they had the horse's 'Neigh'.

The animals stared in disbelief,
Could there be some mistake?
They had to take the vote again,
And started with the snake
Who voted a resounding 'Yess-ss-ss!'
The pig grunted 'OK',
The little lemur said 'Aye-aye!'
But again the horse said, 'Neigh!'

Once more they tried, and this time
The lion paced the floor,
He glared in anger at the horse
As he gave his positive roar,
The donkey gave his ass-ent
With a loud and lusty bray,
But when they all turned to the horse,
He hoarsely whispered 'Neigh'.

'Don't you like the elephant?
Is he not strong and kind!
Is it his size that bothers you?
Is it his small behind?
Perhaps you want someone colourful,
D'you object because he's grey?
Would you like someone else?' they asked.
The horse happily bellowed, 'Neigh!'

The hyena laughed with crazy joy,
The others were exultant,
The cautious cat asked, 'Does this mean
You accept the elephant?'
Horse nodded fast and furiously,
They all shouted, 'Hooray!'
But when they came to vote again,
The horse's vote was – 'Neigh'.

They had to abandon the ballot then,
(According to the rule),
The elephant climbed down off the throne,
(A makeshift bamboo stool).
They cancelled the coronation feast,
As he watched them take the hay,
The horse hung his head in sorrow,
And sadly murmured 'Neigh'.

So the animals went home kingless,
And (it's not widely known, of course),
The elephant, to this moment,
Is not fond of the horse.
Concerning that fiasco,
The horse would like to say,
He's not to blame, although he's tried,
He can't say aught but 'Neigh'.

(He'd like to say it, but of course, he can't.)

Dis Breeze

Dis breeze is a air conditioner,
Dis breeze better than any fan,
Dis breeze blow soft an' warm
Dry me face an' foot an' han.

Dis breeze don't have no manners,
Dis breeze is much too bold,
Look how dis breeze lift up me skirt
And show me knickers to de world!

The Aviary

The signal comes and all at once,
The birds begin their aerial dance,
The skylarks lead the steep ascent,
Arrowing upwards till at length,
They halt and hover, plummet, bank,
And rise again, their numbers ranked
In size and shape, they do this thrice,
The fourth time birds of paradise,
Swifts and swallows, tits, peafowls,
Mews and curlews, pipits, owls,
Starlings, sparrows, whippoorwills,
Merles and orioles, razorbills,
Birds of every size and hue,
Skim swift as thought towards the blue,
They stop as one, turn and swoop
Earthward, float, and loop the loop,
Then spiral heavenwards again,
To form a feathered daisy-chain,
Below, the ostrich and her chicks
Follow the gyring aerobatics
Drum counterpoint to the dulcet fluting,
Till like a host of parachuting
Painted balls they drop to perch
On walls, on branch of ash and birch.

The keeper finds them silent, still,
And worries that his birds are ill.

Don' Go Ova Dere

Barry madda tell 'im
But Barry wouldn' hear,
Barry fada warn 'im
But Barry didn' care.
'Don' go ova dere, bwoy,
Don' go ova dere.'

Barry sista beg 'im
Barry pull her hair,
Barry brother bet 'im
'You can't go ova dere.'
'I can go ova dere, bwoy,
I can go ova dere.'

Barry get a big bag,
Barry climb de gate,
Barry granny call 'im
But Barry couldn' wait,
'Im wan' get ova dere, bwoy,
Before it get too late.

Barry see de plum tree
'Im didn' see de bull,
Barry thinkin' 'bout de plums
'Gwine get dis big bag full.'
De bull get up an' shake, bwoy,
An gi' de rope a pull.

De rope slip off de pole
But Barry didn't see,
De bull begin to stretch 'im foot dem
Barry climb de tree.
Barry start fe eat, bwoy,
Firs' one, den two, den three.

Barry nearly full de bag
An' den 'im hear a soun',
Barry hole de plum limb tight
An' start fe look aroun',
When 'im see de bull, bwoy,
'Im nearly tumble down.

Night a come, de bull naw move
From unda dat plum tree,
Barry madda wondering
Whey Barry coulda be.
Barry getting tired, bwoy,
Of sitting in dat tree.

An' Barry dis realise
'Im neva know before,
Sey de tree did full o' black ants
But now 'im know fe sure,
For some begin fe bite 'im, bwoy,
Den more, an' more, an' more.

De bull lay down fe wait it out
An' Barry mek a jump,
De bag o' plum drop out de tree
An' Barry hear a thump,
By early de nex' mawnin' bwoy,
Dat bull gwine have a lump.

De plum so frighten dat po' bull
'Im start fe run too late,
'Im a gallop afta Barry
But Barry jump de gate,
De bull jus' stamp 'im foot, bwoy,
'Im yeye dem full o' hate.

When Barry ketch a 'im yard,
What a state 'im in!
'Im los' 'im bag, 'im clothes mud up
An mud deh pon 'im chin,
An whey de black ants bite 'im
Feba bull-frog skin.

Barry fada spank 'im,
'Im madda sey 'im sin,
Barry sista scold 'im,
But Barry only grin,
For Barry brother shake 'im head
An' sey, 'Barry, yuh win!'

Chicken Poxed

My sister was spotty,
Real spotty all over,
She was plastered with spots
From her head to her toes.

She had spots on the parts
That her bathing suits cover,
Spots on her eyelids,
Spots on her nose.

I didn't know chickenpox
Could be so interesting,
It seemed such a shame
To waste all those spots.

So when Jody was sleeping
And no one was looking,
I got a blue pen
And connected her dots.

Fear of Ghosts

How old are you? he said.
I'm three, how old are you? she said.
I'm dead. Aren't you afraid of me? he said.
Don't be absurd, if you are dead
How can you speak to me? she said.
And where's your head?

Here, underneath my arm, you see?
And now perhaps you will agree
You really should be scared of me,
Be shivering in your bed, he said.
It must be really weird, she said,
To wear your head so awkwardly,
How do you see?

My eyes are in my head, he said,
Where they should be.
See how they glow bright ruby red,
Look how my body on your bedspread
Has left no mark for you to see,
The doors are locked, I have no key,
Yet I come in. And tell me, Leigh,
Did you hear tread of feet on the stairhead
Before you saw me?
You really should be filled with dread,
For I'm a ghost, you see.

Mum says there are no ghosts, she said.
I am a ghost, I'm newly dead,
I need to scare children, he said,
A minimum of three
Before they'll let me enrol
In the Royal Ghost Society.

There are no ghosts, she quietly said,
Now I would like to go to bed,
So kindly take your glowing head
And go sit on the settee.

I think I'll take my leave, he said
For it is plain to see
As long as you're alive and I am dead
We two will not agree.
I'll go away and haunt instead
Some other child who's more well-bred,
Who'll not contradict me.

He quickly rose, put on his head,
And in a puff of smoke, he fled
Into the dark chimney.

Goodnight, she said.

The Hyena

The hyena has neither charm nor wit.
Beauty and courage? He hasn't a bit,
In the animal world he has no clout,
So I don't know what he's laughing about.

Christmas Carol

Dress the walls with casuarina
Flaming red poinsettia too,
Mix among them alamanda,
Hibiscus of countless hues
Snow-on-the-mountain, poinciana,
Christmas candles 'cross the door.
Pink and purple bougainvillea,
For it's Christmas-time once more.

Pick the sorrel from the stalk now,
It's that special time of year,
Reap the swollen ginger root and
Make the special ginger beer,
Tangerines are ripe and juicy,
Sweet oranges by the score,
Dig the yams, they'll now be ready,
For it's Christmas-time once more.

The Christmas Tree

The Christmas tree is in from the forest,
Standing by the window, out of the cold,
She's wearing a necklace of stars and spangles,
And her fingers are covered in rings of gold.

Her foot's encased in sparkling silver,
There are party streamers, and perhaps more
Than a hundred lights winking in her hair.
Presents stacked high on the floor

Underneath her shimmering skirt,
Her bells and baubles bob and sway,
Like a queen she smiles in silence,
Is it the Christmas tree's birthday?

Cane Flags

Cane flags are growing, Christmas is near,
Cane flags are waving, it's the end of the year,
Cane flags are dying, harvest is here,
When men with machetes come, cane flags disappear.

The River

The River's a wanderer,
A nomad, a tramp,
He doesn't choose one place
To set up his camp.

The River's a winder,
Through valley and hill
He twists and he turns,
He just cannot be still.

The River's a hoarder,
And he buries down deep
Those little treasures
That he wants to keep.

The River's a baby,
He gurgles and hums,
And sounds like he's happily
Sucking his thumbs.

The River's a singer,
As he dances along,
The countryside echoes
The notes of his song.

The River's a monster
Hungry and vexed,
He's gobbled up trees
And he'll swallow you next.

Pinda Cake

De pinda cake lady comin' down'
With her basket an' glass case she comin' to town,
She stop by de school gate an' set up her stall,
An' while she a-set up, hear de old lady bawl:

Pinda! Pinda cake!
Pinda! Pinda cake!
Gal an' bwoy me jus' done bake,
Come buy yuh lovely pinda cake!

She have grater cake an' she have duckunoo,
Coconut drops an' bulla cake too,
Jackass corn an' plantain tart,
But the t'ing dat dearest to me heart

Is Pinda! Pinda cake!
Pinda! Pinda cake!
Gal an' bwoy me jus' done bake,
Come buy yuh lovely pinda cake!

We all crowd round her an' yuh can tell
By de look o' de cake dem, an' de spicy smell
Dat they won't stay in de glass case too long,
As we buy from de lady, we join in de song.

Pinda! Pinda cake!
Pinda! Pinda cake!
Gal an' bwoy me jus' done bake,
Come buy yuh lovely pinda cake!

If

If only my head wasn't heavy as lead
And that glow didn't come from this floor,
If I wasn't so nervy, my mind topsy-turvy,
And there wasn't a shadow on the door,
If my ears didn't hear and my eyes didn't stare at
Things no one else hears or sees,
If the dogs didn't bark, if outside wasn't dark
And I didn't have the shakes in my knees,
If I wasn't so sure that that ear-splitting snore
Couldn't have come from anyone who's alive,
If my heart didn't leap, if my 'flesh' didn't creep
And I was certain this night I'd survive,
If this night weren't so long, if that low mournful song
Didn't freeze every thought in my brain,
If I could be assured that the scuttling I heard
Was only the rats in the drain,
If that shape that I see was the branch of a tree
A shadow cast by the cloud-shrouded moon,
If I could understand why it looks like a hand
Conducting some unearthly tune,
If all that I've said were just in my head
And the whole thing weren't so daunting,
I could return to my grave, feeling ever so brave,
And quite satisfied with my first haunting.

Why Is It?

Why is it that the taps all drip,
The electricity wires trip,
Tired pipes in the attic grumble,
Empty washer-dryers tumble,
Floorboards creak and old joints moan,
Doorposts squeak and rafters groan,
Fridges softly hum and sigh,
Cats out in the garden cry
Like a band of mad banshees,
The wind howls eerily in the trees,
The telephone rings, there's no one there,
There are soft whispers in the air,
The moon starts playing hide and seek,
Your head feels light, your knees feel weak,
You think you're not alone in bed,
And wish you were elsewhere instead.

When you're alone at night?

Acceptance

Thank you for asking me over to tea,
I'm pleased to accept, that'll be grand,
But I feel I must warn you, certain foods don't like me,
And one or two foods I can't stand.

I expect you know I'm a vegetarian, so
Meat, fish and poultry are out,
I eat most vegetables, except one or two
Like pepper, tomato and sprout.

I'm not terribly keen on turnips or swedes,
And onions disrupt my inside,
And please don't use garlic if you're cooking for me,
For the smell I just cannot abide.

I can't stand all that exotic stuff,
I hope you don't think I'm boring,
But I find those rich sauces, and pasta and rice
Are too apt to send my weight soaring.

Potatoes are lovely (not roasted or fried),
Though they do tend to keep me awake,
I can't say I've liked any sweet that I've tried,
So, no pastry, ice cream or cake.

For some reason regretfully, I cannot eat fruits,
Something I admit I find trying,
But with sensitive stomachs just as with spilt milk,
I've found it's no use at all crying.

Oh, I don't use milk, eggs, butter or cheese,
My delicate constitution you see,
Apart from that I eat anything at all,
I look forward to coming to tea.

When I Grow Up and Have Children

When I grow up and have children,
And they ask if they can use the phone,
I'll tell them, 'You can't, if you want to call someone
You'll have to buy a phone of your own.'

When I grow up and have children,
And they ask if they can stay up late,
I'll say, 'You can't, even if you're eighteen,
You must be asleep by eight.'

When I grow up and have children,
And they ask if they can play in the street,
I'll say, 'No, you can't, what more do you want,
We've the backyard, that square of concrete.'

And when my children get angry and cry,
I'll ask them, 'What can I do?
I learnt everything I know from my Mum',
That's right, I'll blame it on you.

Ah Was Readin' a Book

Ah was readin' a book about chestnut,
An' me start wonder as me a-read,
If dem roast the chestnut the same way
That we roast we jackfruit seed.

Ah was readin' a book about daffodil,
An' a thought jus' come into me head,
Yuh think the daffodil look like we mimosa,
Only yellow, instead of red?

Ah was readin' a book about motorway,
Long, wide road that don't have much ben',
An' ah wonder if them was anyt'ing like
The road between Kingston an' May Pen.

Ah was readin' a book about the Queen,
An' ah think, it would be funny,
If the English queen was a warrior,
Like we own maroon queen, Nanny.

Ah was readin' a book about England,
An' a stop an' wonder for a minute,
If a English girl have a book 'bout Jamaica,
An' if a little girl like me was in it.

Criminal Record

You've got a criminal record,
Wanted for assault,
Guilty of causing a racket,
And it's time you called a halt.

You've got a criminal record,
Stop that yelling, cease the din,
That's a criminal record you've got there,
So throw it in the bin.

New Baby

Me baby sista come home las' week,
An' bwoy, me nearly dead
When Mama pull back de blanket
An' me see de pickney head!

Couple piece o' hair she have pon it,
An' de little pickney face
Wrinkle up an' crease up so,
Like she did have it in a suitcase.

Me see her a chew up Mama chest,
So me give her piece o' meat,
Mama take it 'way, say she can't eat yet,
For she no have no teet'.

Me tell Mama to put her down,
Make she play with me blue van,
She say Yvonne can't sit or stand up yet,
Nor hold things in her han'.

Me say, all right, but maybe
She can play 'I spy' with me,
She tell me the pickney can't talk yet,
And she can hardly see.

Although she no have no use,
And she teck over me little bed,
Me wouldn't mind so much if she never
Make so much noise in me head.

Every night she wake me up,
But a Mama me sorry fah,
For every time she wake up,
She start to eat Mama.

She blind, she dumb, she ugly, she bald,
She smelly, she can't understan',
Ah wish Mama would take her back,
An' buy one different one.

My Sister ...

My sister's going to cop it,
She's thrown food on the floor,
She's overturned her cup and now,
She's banging on the door,
She's scrunched up that last doughnut
And is yelling out for more,
I think that she's in trouble now for sure.

My sister's breaking pencils,
Spreading playdough on her head,
She's thrown Teddy out the window
Into Mum's new flower bed,
She's scribbled on the telly
With crayons, purple and red,
I think that she'll be sent straight to her bed.

My sister's in the bath and
There are soapsuds everywhere,
The carpet's gone all soggy
And she doesn't even care,
She filled the plastic bucket,
Emptied it over her hair,
When Daddy comes she'd better hide somewhere.

My sister threw her bricks about
And hit Dad on his knee,
But he just smiled and patted her,
Now she's playing happily,
After all that she has done,
She's getting off scot free,
I wonder – would it work the same for me?

... My Brother

My brother is in trouble
And he's been sent to bed,
He didn't know he shouldn't
Plaster jelly on his head,
He didn't know that daddies
Don't like being hit with bricks,
And what's cute when you are two
Is just plain naughty when you're six.

Sun a-shine, Rain a-fall

Sun a-shine an' rain a-fall,
The Devil an' him wife cyan 'gree at all,
The two o' them want one fish-head,
The Devil call him wife bonehead,
She hiss her teeth, call him cockeye,
Greedy, worthless an' workshy,
While them busy callin' name,
The puss walk in, sey is a shame
To see a nice fish go to was'e,
Lef' with a big grin pon him face.

You Should Try It

'I'm giving you this slice of pie,' he said,
'It's the very last slice on the plate,
My very best dessert is peach pie,
But I'm giving it to you 'cause you're great.

It's a present, a gift, a small token,' he said,
'A thank you for all you have done,
You have the last slice of my fresh-baked peach pie,
I'll nibble this stale currant bun.'

'Are you really quite sure about this?' I asked,
My eyes watering with desire for that slice,
And I thought how snugly it would nestle
In my stomach on the bed of fried rice.

'Absolutely,' he said, 'don't you mind me,
You deserve it, it's yours, have it all,'
As I prepared to take my first bite,
He turned his face to the wall.

He shivered and twitched, I munched, licked my lips,
He groaned as I swallowed each mouthful,
I couldn't help thinking that performance of his,
Was not in the smallest bit tactful.

He waited until I had finished then asked
In the doleful voice of a foghorn,
'How was it? Was it nice?' 'Delicious!' I said,
'You should try it, oh sorry, all gone.'

Chicken Dinner

Mama, don' do it, please
Don' cook that chicken fe dinner,
We know that chicken from she hatch
She is the only one in the batch
That the mangoose didn't catch,
Please don' cook her fe dinner.

Mama, don't do it, please,
Don' cook that chicken fe dinner,
Yuh mean to tell me yuh feget
Yuh promise her to we as a pet?
She not even have a chance fe lay yet
And yuh want fe cook her fe dinner.

Mama, don' do it, please,
Don' cook that chicken fe dinner,
Don't give Henrietta the chop,
I tell yuh what, we could swap
We will get yuh one from the shop
If yuh promise not to cook her fe dinner.

Mama, me really glad yuh know
That yuh never cook Henny fe dinner,
And she really glad too, I bet,
Oh Lawd, me suddenly feel upset.
Yuh don' suppose is somebody else pet
We eating now fe dinner?

In the Car Park

They shouldn't be allowed out in public!
It's a disgrace!
Just look at that fender!
Have you ever seen so much rust in your life?
Quite puts you off your oil, that does.
Suppose it's all you can expect really.
Take a look at the human he drives!
A poet, no doubt!
Or a vicar. A teacher you think?
Oh dear! No wonder he's in such a state.
D'you know, those teachers will wait till you're
On your last litre before they'll go into
A petrol station.
They're as poor as a beggar with holes in his pockets.
I knew a Rover who had his insides
Wrecked from lack of sustenance.
He ended up crippled in the middle of the road.
Can you imagine the disgrace!
He used to drive a headmaster!

Me, I wouldn't swap my pop star for all the oil in Arabia.
Mind you, he does abuse my brakes something terrible.
And the way he spins my wheel sometimes, it makes me
    dizzy.

So what kind of person do you drive then?
A politician, eh! Well! I bet you've got some tales to tell!

Oh, there's that Jaguar we met at the Proms last week.
Toot, toot! There's a space over here! C'mon, make
    yourself small.
Well! Some vehicles! Pretending he hadn't heard. Not
    good enough for him, I suppose.
Huh!
Well, let him go and talk to that stuck-up Rolls if he likes.
They're no better than each other is what I say.
Ooh! Look who's heading this way!
Spread out, spread out!
We don't want her sort over here.
I'd die if anyone saw me in company with a Ford!
Oh, thank goodness! Here's my person now.
I guess there'll be no keeping that sad car out now.
Sorry to leave you with her, but I think it's time
For my wash and wax. See you around.
Toot, toot!

Tables

Headmaster a come, mek has'e! Sit down!
Jo, mind yuh bruck Jane collar bone.
Tom, tek yuh foot off o' de desk,
Sandra Wallace, mi know yuh vex
But beg yuh get off o' Joseph head.
Tek de lizard off o' Sue neck, Ted!
Sue, mi dear, don' bawl so loud,
Thomas, why yuh put de toad
Eena Elvira sandwich bag?
Jim what yuh gwine do wid dat bull-frog?
Tek it off mi chair, yuh mad?
Yuh chair small, May, but it not dat bad
Dat yuh haffe siddung pon de floor!
Jim, don' squeeze de frog unda de door
Put it through de window – no, no, Les!
Mi know yuh hungry, but Mary yeas
Won' fill yuh up, so spit it out.
Now go wash de blood out o' yuh mout'.
Hortense, tek Mary to de nurse.
Nick, tek yuh han' outa Mary purse
Ah wonda who tell all o' yuh
Sey dat dis classroom is a zoo?
Quick! Headmaster comin' through de door.
'Two ones are two, two twos are four.'

Sly Mangoose

Mangoose creep up by the kitchen
Trying to catch the little chicken,
Him didn't see the mother hen,
Mangoose won't try do that agen.

Chickens Come from Eggs

Chickens come from eggs,
A mosquito from a larva,
Tadpoles come from frogspawn,
And fleas from my dog Rover.

Meck Me Play

Meck me play with yuh dolly,
Meck me comb her hair,
Meck me play with yuh dolly, do,
Meck me pick the dress she wear?

Me will give yuh a taste o' me mango,
Me will meck yuh drive me car,
If yuh meck me play with yuh dolly,
Me wi gi' yuh piece o' me chocolate bar.

Meck me play with yuh dolly,
Meck me bathe her, please
Meck me play with yuh dolly,
Meck me kiss her an' give her a squeeze.

Me will just touch her face real soft,
Ah won' break her again, OK?
Yuh won't meck me play with yuh dolly?
Cho, she too ugly anyway.

Riddle 1

In springtime when new buds are seen,
I wear a dress of sparkling green,
In summer when the days are mellow,
I wear a dress of green and yellow,
In autumn, crimson, gold and brown,
Are the colours in my gown,
But when the snows begin to fall,
I don't wear any clothes at all.

Riddle 2

When I was born, I had two horns,
But as I grew I lost them,
With age my face put on some fat,
And sparkled as a bright gem.

As I got old, I lost the fat,
Became very thin, and then
Just before I passed away,
I grew my horns again.

(Answer 2: the moon)
(Answer 1: a tree)

Following John About

Hi, I'm Alan, pleased to meet you,
Sorry, can't stop, I'm a scout,
And my good deed for today
Is to follow John about.

This is John, say hello John,
John just loves to scream and shout,
At the moment John is screaming,
'I said don't follow me about!'

John's my brother, older brother,
Calls me names like 'Sprog' and 'Sprout',
But I know how to get my own back,
I just follow him about.

John's been fishing in the river,
All day long, and he's caught nowt,
I've not seen him look so gloomy
Since I've been following him about.

Here's a fish, fresh caught this morning,
John says it's salmon, I think it's trout,
Saw him buy it in the market
When I followed him about.

John is madder than a march hare,
Says that I had best watch out,
'Cause I told Mum 'bout the fish,
And followed him about.

Bye now, can't stop, in a hurry,
I'm just trying to dodge a clout,
I don't think this is a good time
To be following John about.

Tell Me a Story

Tell me a story please, Granny,
'Bout Anancy and Tacoma,
Or tell me the one 'bout Brer Rabbit,
Brer Dog and Brer Tiger.

Tell me a story, meck me 'fraid,
'Bout Ole Haig an' Rollin' Calf,
Or tell me 'bout Brer Rat an' Puss
An' meck me dead wid laugh.

Tell me 'bout when de baby born,
'Bout de t'ree wise men,
Ah know ah hear it plenty time,
But ah want to hear it again.

Tell me a story, please, Granny,
Look how de moon shine bright,
She shining so, because she know,
Is story time tonight.

Tell me a story, please, Granny,
Tell me 'bout t'ree finger Jack,
Tell me a story, tell me a story,
Tell me a sto–

Crick!

CRACK!

Water Everywhere

There's water on the ceiling,
And water on the wall,
There's water in the bedroom,
And water in the hall,
There's water on the landing,
And water on the stair,
Whenever Daddy takes a bath
There's water everywhere.

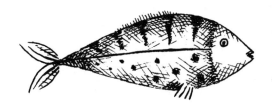

Mega Star Rap

I'm the king of the keyboard, star of the screen,
They call me Gamesmaster, you know what I mean,
'Cause I am just ace on the Nintendo action,
When I get in my stride, you know, I don't give a fraction,
With Super Mario I'm a real daredevil,
I'm cool, I'm wicked, on a different level!
I'll take on anyone who wants to challenge me,
No matter what the problem is, I hold the key.
I can tell you every shortcut on the Megadrive,
I can put the Sonic Hedgehog into overdrive,
And I would, I really would like to accept your dare,
But I've just run out of batteries for my Sega Game Gear.

Flunked

'Write on one of the following,' my teacher said,
'Gases, solids, water vapour.'
I failed the test, because instead,
I chose to write on paper.

Toast

I've got toast in my navel,
Toast between my toes,
I've even got toast on my head,
I've got toast in my armpits,
Toast in my nose,
That's the last time I eat toast in bed.

The Jackass Lame

Sey yuh want to tease the jackass?
No, him won't kick, him lame tonight.
Wha' wrong with yuh now? Oh, me feget
To tell yuh that the jackass bite.

Leave Dem Wasp Alone

Leave dem wasp alone, Barry,
Leave dem wasp alone.

One pile o' stone beside Barry,
And over Barry head,
Some wasp dere makin' nest
And Barry want to see them dead.

Leave dem wasp alone, Barry,
Leave dem wasp alone.

Over to the right o' Barry
Is a deep blue pool,
Over to the left o' Barry
Is the infant school.

Leave dem wasp alone, Barry,
Leave dem wasp alone.

Barry fling a big stone
And dive into the pool,
The wasp dem trying to sting Barry
But Barry keeping cool.

Leave dem wasp alone, Barry,
Leave dem wasp alone.

As the wasp dem settle down
Barry start crawl out
Barry looking roun' to see
If anyone about.

Leave dem wasp alone, Barry,
Leave dem wasp alone.

Barry fling the next stone
And jump into the water,
The wasp dem chasing Barry
Mother, father, son and daughter.

Leave dem wasp alone, Barry,
Leave dem wasp alone.

Well the wasp dem really vex,
Dem fly over the pool,
But Barry keep him head down,
Barry keeping cool.

Leave dem wasp alone, Barry,
Leave dem wasp alone.

Barry climb out o' the pool,
As the wasp dem settle dung,
Barry look around
And pick a stone up off the grung.

Leave dem wasp alone, Barry,
Leave dem wasp alone.

Barry fling the next stone
And hop into the pool,
Look like the wasp dem want to learn,
Dem heading for the school.

Leave dem wasp alone, Barry,
Leave dem wasp alone.

Hear the pickney dem a-scream,
Hear the teacher shout,
See the wasp dem wreck the class
Drive everybody out.

Leave dem wasp alone, Barry,
Leave dem wasp alone.

Teacher send home all o' dem,
The pickney them a-cry,
Barry laughing so hard now
That water fill him yeye.

Leave dem wasp alone, Barry,
Leave dem wasp alone.

Barry fling the next stone
Him heading fe the pool,
Barry meet the group o' wasp dem
Coming from the school.

Leave dem wasp alone, Barry,
Leave dem wasp alone.

Barry running down the road
The wasp dem backa him,
People think is jogging
Barry jogging to keep trim.

Leave dem wasp alone, Barry,
Leave dem wasp alone.

Watch poor Barry going home,
Whole heap o' coco pon him head,
Watch the wasp dem laughing
As dem fly back home to bed.

Sprouting Bougainvillea Stump

Two pin-pricks of purple,
She swore to me were leaves,
Two pinpricks of purple.
No one would believe
The joy those pinpricks gave her,
The way she smiled all day,
She was happy as a proud new mother,
With her newborn on display.
Two tiny pricks of purple,
No one could ever love,
Except of course, my mother,
And the gardener up above.

Troilet (London Spires)

London spires, tall and stately,
Hold their heads above the fog,
Around the world admired greatly,
London spires tall and stately,
Keep on dreaming so sedately
Languid in the choking smog.
London spires tall and stately,
Hold their heads above the fog.

Enjoy the Party

I went to a party in Shepherd's Wood,
I'm telling you, man, that food looked good.

I'm reaching out for a chicken leg,
When a man comes up and says, 'I beg

Your pardon, don't think me rude,
But you ought to know before you eat this food,

That it could be bad for your well being,
I thought it my duty to warn you, seeing

That chicken might be full of antibiotics,
You might think I'm just being neurotic

But do you know where that pork comes from?
D'you know how much preservatives went into that ham?

The beef could give you CJD,
You wouldn't touch it if you were me.

Yes, I think it's a brilliant plan,
Give up that meat, go vegetarian.

Although apples are waxed and oranges dyed
Soya bean is genetically modified,

I've heard of carrots that make teeth glow,
There's toxin in potato skins, you know.

You'll just have a drink? Well watch your spleen,
Alcohol is a drug, so I wouldn't be so keen

To take it. Spring water? That's an idea,
Though careful, it doesn't take a seer

To know the pollutants that are found
In bottled water seep into the ground

From pesticides and things like that.
Well, I've enjoyed our little chat.'

He left with a smile that was sour as lime,
Throwing over his shoulder, 'Have a good time.'

The Expert

I know the workings of the ant,
Its anatomy and psychology,
I'm an authority on the ant,
An expert in anthology.

The Pig

You really are a silly shape,
They all said to the pig,
Your beady eyes are much too small,
Your snout is much too big.
It is a mystery to us
How you get up off the ground
With all that blubber you insist
On carrying around,
Your neck is hardly there at all,
You should hide it with a scarf,
Your tail is like a corkscrew
And you have a stupid laugh,
It really is no wonder
You are only fit for spam,

The pig snorted from his muddy bed,
I ham just what I ham.

The Cricket's Lament

The flea's a world-class athlete,
He's the greatest long-jumper I know,
The butterfly's dressed in the brightest and boldest
Colours of the rainbow.

The scorpion has a sting in his tail
That's the talk of every town,
The caterpillar's wriggling body
Is as soft as eiderdown.

There's nothing quite as tasty,
As the honey made by the bee,
So what is a cricket's claim to fame?
I've got me ears in me knee!

Peeny-Wally

Day jus' done an' night a-fall,
Peeny-wally pon di wall,
Wid him lamp fe show de way,
Peeny-wally never stray.

Sun wake up, drive 'way de night,
Peeny-wally out him light,
By de time de mawnin' come,
Peeny-wally fly gawn home.

Henry the Eighth

Henry the Eighth had six wives,
The reason was quite strange,
It wasn't that he loved them all,
He just loved to chop and change.

Teatime

Take two teaspoons, take two teacups,
Take two teabags too,
Tip the teabags in the teapot,
Time for tea for two.

The Queen is Coming

Mop the floors and make the beds,
Shine the windows, clean the sheds,
Let's have the smell of fresh-baked bread,
The queen is coming to visit.

Pave the roads and clear the drains,
Paint the buses, buy new trains,
Cover the stadium in case it rains,
The queen is coming to visit.

Cut the hedges, sweep the streets,
Purchase mortar and concrete,
We have new buildings to complete,
The queen is coming to visit.

Don't you mention the recession,
Or you'll be sacked for indiscretion,
We want to give a good impression,
The queen is coming to visit.

Move the squatters, move their shacks,
In the space, erect some plaques,
Arrest objectors, we don't want flak,
The queen is coming to visit.

Gag the loudmouths, troublemakers,
Close the bars and the bookmakers,
Let's be sober as undertakers,
The queen is coming to visit.

Line the roads with flowers and streamers,
Hide the beggars, loafers, dreamers,
The higglers and the roadside screamers,
The queen is coming to visit.

Get the guitars, fifes and drums,
Get the choir, here she comes,
Now smile, come, show those teeth and gums,
The queen is coming to visit.

Wave those banners, shout hooray!
Where's that child with the bouquet?
This is a very special day,
The queen is coming to visit.

Well that was short, but it was sweet.
You only saw her hands and feet?
Well she couldn't hang around in this heat,
It was only a fleeting visit.

Warning

Quick, Nick!
Mind the brick!
Too late,
Broken pate.

De
(Inspired by Thomas Hood's poem 'No')

De snow, de sleet, de lack o' heat,
De wishy-washy sunlight,
De lip turn blue, de cold, 'ACHOO!'
De runny nose, de frostbite,

De creakin' knee, de misery,
De joint dem all rheumatic,
De icy bed (de blanket dead),
De burs' pipe in de attic.

De window a-shake, de glass near break,
De wind dat cut like razor,
De wonderin' why you never buy
De window from dat double-glazer.

De heavy coat, zip to de throat,
De nose an' ears all pinky,
De weepin' sky, de clothes can't dry,
De day dem long an' inky.

De icy road, de heavy load,
De las' minute Christmus shoppin'
De cuss an' fret 'cause you feget
De ribbon an' de wrappin'.

De mud, de grime, de slush, de slime,
De place gloomy, since November,
De sinkin' heart, is jus' de start, o'
De wintertime,
December.

Glossary

ah	I
a-go	is/was going (*a-* before a word takes the place of *-ing* in standard English)
bruck	break
bulla cake	small, round, spiced cake eaten as a snack
burs'/bus	burst
bwoy	boy
callaloo	leafy vegetable, used like spinach
cho	interjection of disgust, irritation, impatience, scepticism or scorn
cho-cho	vegetable from the marrow family
coco	lump on the head from a blow or an insect bite
coconut drops	diced coconut cooked in spiced caramel
cole	cold
cyan	can't/cannot
dah/dat	that
dawg	dog
de	the
deh/dere	there
dem	them
den	then
dis	this
doah	door
doan/don'	don't
dose	those
duckunoo	sweet made from grated corn, spice, coconut cream and sugar, wrapped in banana leaves and boiled
dung	down
duppy	ghost
eena	in

ef	if
fada	father
fah	for
feba	(favour) resemble(s)
fe	for/to
fee-fee	a vine which blooms at Christmas time – the purple and white flowers are sucked to produce a high-pitched whistle
feget	forget
fubba-fubba	fruit wrinkled and tasteless from being picked while still unfit and forced to ripen
gal	girl
galang	go on/go along
gat	got/have
gawn	gone
gi'	give
grater cake	sweet made from grated coconut, spice and sugar
grung	ground
gwan	go on
gwine	going
hag	hog/pig
halla	holler/cry
has'e	haste
hole	hold
i'	it
ile	oil
'im	him/he/his
jackass corn	large flat biscuit made from grated coconut, flour, bicarbonate of soda and spice
jonkunnu	masked street dancers and musicians who perform as part of the Christmas celebrations
ketch	catch/reach

lef'	leave/left
likkle	little
lissen	listen
los'	lost
madda	mother
massa	master/mister
mawnin'	morning
me	I
meck/mek	make
mi	me/my
min'	mind
naw	not
neva	never
noh	not
nowhey	nowhere
nuff	plenty/many
nutten	nothing
o'	of
odder	other
outa doah	outside/outdoors
ova	over
peeny-wally/wallie	firefly/fireflies
pickney	child
pinda cake	sugar cake with peanuts
pon	on/upon
quatty	a half penny in old currency, now used to mean a few pence/cents
run-dung	sauce made from coconut cream and seasoning, usually cooked with meat or fish
sah	sir
sey	say
shet	shut/close
siddung	sit (down)
soun'	sound
starlight	sparkler(s)

'tan	stay/stand
teck	take
ting	thing
to-to	small, sweet cake
tru	through
trus	give/take goods on credit
unda	under
unoo	plural form of you
wan'	want
wha	what
whey	where
wid	with
wile	wild
winda	window
yeas	ear/ears
yeye	eye/eyes
eye-water	tears
yuh	you